D0528379

The Little Book

of

ONE-LINERS

The Little Book
of
ONE-LINERS

Edited by

ALISON BULLIVANT

mustard

First published in 1999 by Mustard
Mustard is an imprint of Parragon

Parragon
Queen Street House
4 Queen Street
Bath BA1 1HE UK

Produced by Magpie Books, an imprint of
Robinson Publishing Ltd, London

Cover illustration courtesy of Superstock

ISBN 1 84164 196 0

A copy of the British Library Cataloguing-in-Publication Data
is available from the British Library

Contents

Introduction

Noah was an amateur; the Titanic was built by professionals.

Malcolm Allison

Brilliant conversation was once an art and those with talent (Samuel Johnson, Oscar Wilde, Dorothy Parker, to name but a very few) produced some masterpieces. The Little Book of One-Liners contains a variety of snippets ranging from the subtly clever to the vitriolic. And not only do we admire alacrity of wit but there is something about the human race that draws great amusement from the verbal slaying of others. Perhaps it is the modern equivalent of watching the Christians thrown to the lions. This collection of wicked understatement and abusive oratory should satisfy the most voracious appetite.

Chapter 1

ARTISTIC TEMPERAMENT

Michael Caine can out-act any, well nearly any, telephone kiosk you care to mention.

Hugh Leonard

Stage and screen, music, art and literature — more inventive invective and critical commentary from those in the limelight.

They couldn't direct lemmings off a cliff.

Doug Brod

Boy George is all England needs – another queen who can't dress.

Joan Rivers

Edward Woodward – his name sounds like someone farting in the bath.

Noël Coward

I'd have sex with sand before I'd have sex with Roseanne.

Howard Stern

~⋅⦂⦂⋅~

He looks like a half-melted rubber bulldog.

John Simon (of Walter Matthau)

~⋅⦂⦂⋅~

Joan Collins is a commodity who would sell her own bowel movement.

Anthony Newley (of his ex-wife)

~⋅⦂⦂⋅~

Like a rat up a rope.

Coral Browne (of a hyperactive colleague)

The Henry Fondas lay on the evening like a damp Mackintosh.

Noël Coward

Bambi with testosterone.

Owen Glieberman (of Prince)

A swaggering tough little slut.

Louise Brooks (of Shirley Temple)

Audrey Hepburn is a walking X-ray.

Billy Wilder

Wet she was a star – dry she ain't.
                    Joe Pasternak (of swimmer turned actress
                    Esther Williams)

Like acting with 210 pounds of condemned veal.
                    Coral Browne (of a male actor)

If I found her floating in my pool, I'd punish my dog.
                    Joan Rivers (of Yoko Ono)

She was like a sinking ship, firing on the rescuers.
Alexander Woollcott (of Mrs Patrick Campbell)

Mick Jagger is about as sexy as a pissing toad.
Truman Capote

Tallulah Bankhead barged down the Nile last night as Cleopatra – and sank.
John Mason Brown

His features resemble a fossilized washrag.
Alan Brien (of Steve McQueen)

A testicle with legs.
Pauline Kael (of Bob Hoskins)

Barbara Cartland's eyes were twin miracles of mascara and looked like two small crows that had crashed into a chalk cliff.

Clive James

Madonna's so hairy – when she lifted her arm I thought it was Tina Turner in her armpit.

Joan Rivers

She has only two things going for her – a father and a mother.

John Simon (of Liza Minnelli)

Los Angeles – the plastic asshole of the world.

William Faulkner

Hollywood – they know only one word of more than one syllable here, and that is *fillum*.

Louis Sherwin

If Woody Allen didn't exist then somebody would have knitted him.

Lesley White

Hollywood – a trip through a sewer in a glass-bottomed boat.

Wilson Mizner

They shot too many pictures and not enough actors.

Walter Winchell

~❦~

When I grow up, I still want to be a director.

Steven Spielberg

~❦~

Editing the film *The Boy Friend,* a gorilla in boxing gloves wielding a pair of garden shears could have done a better job.

Ken Russell

~❦~

No picture can hold my interest when the leading man's tits are larger than the leading lady's.

Groucho Marx (of Victor Mature)

Getting the costumes right in *Cleopatra* was like polishing the fish-knives on the Titanic.

> Julian Barnes

Pardon me Ma'am, I thought you were a guy I knew in Pittsburgh.

> Groucho Marx (to Greta Garbo in
> *Bring on the Empty Horses*)

James Cagney rolled through the film like a very belligerent barrel.

> Noël Coward

Like kissing Hitler.

> Tony Curtis (on kissing Marilyn Monroe)

The best time I ever had with Joan (Crawford) was when I pushed her down the stairs in *Whatever Happened to Baby Jane.*

Bette Davis

～·❦·～

Ryan O'Neal is so stiff and clumsy he can't even act a part requiring him to be stiff and clumsy.

Jay Cocks

～·❦·～

Say anything you want about me, but you make fun of my picture and you'll regret it the rest of your fat midget life.

Joshua Logan (to Truman Capote)

This is one of those films that should never have been released – not even on parole.

Christopher Tookey

Nowadays Mitchum doesn't so much act as point his suit at people.

Russell Davies

This film wasn't released – it escaped.

James Caan

And to Hell it can go!

Ed Naha (of the film *From Hell It Came*)

Never judge a book by its movie.

J.W. Eagan

❧

Book: what they make a movie out of for television.

Leonard Louis Levinson

❧

To suggest that *Break A Leg* needs a splint would be to offer it an unjustifiable hope of recovery.

Clive Barnes

❧

Cher looked like a bag of tattooed bones in a sequined slingshot.

Worst Dressed List

Marilyn Monroe was good at playing abstract confusion in the same way that a midget is good at being short.

Clive James

That's what you think!
James Agee (of the film *You Were Meant For Me*)

Television is chewing gum for the mind.

Frank Lloyd Wright

Television: an electric device which, when turned off, stimulates conversation.

Anon

He directed rehearsals with all the airy deftness of a rheumatic deacon producing *Macbeth* for a church social.

Noël Coward (of J.R. Crawford)

I think that first nights should come near the end of a play's run – as indeed they often do.

Peter Ustinov

If they'd stuffed the child's head up the horse's arse, they would have solved two problems at once.

Noël Coward (of Bonnie Langford, after a horse had defecated on stage)

It was misnamed by five.

Alexander Woollcott (of the play *Number Seven*)

The first rule of comedy is not to perform in a town where they still point at aeroplanes.

Bobby Mills

It was one of those plays in which all the actors unfortunately enunciated very clearly.

Robert Benchley

Since the war a terrible pall of significance has fallen over plays.

Noël Coward

You never get a chance to sit down unless you're a king.

Josephine Hull (on acting in Shakespeare's plays)

I suppose I could make changes in my play but who am I to tamper with a masterpiece.

Oscar Wilde

For God's sake go and tell that young man to take that Rockingham tea service out of his tights!

Noël Coward (of a male dancer who
omitted to "gird" himself properly)

In this production of *Macbeth*, the prompter stole the show.

Peter Lewis

The scenery was beautiful but the actors got in front of it.

Alexander Woollcott

It's about as long as *Parsifal*, and not as funny.

Noël Coward (on *Camelot*)

Last time I performed my name was so low on the program I was getting orders for the printing.

Frank Carson

The Blaises were both a bit desiccated and lacked vitality to such a degree that one felt oxygen should be served after the fish.

Noël Coward

He played the King as though under momentary apprehension that someone else was about to play the ace.

Eugene Field (of Creston Clarke)

The press was almost unanimous on one thing, and that was that I should never have been allowed to appear in it.

Noël Coward (of his role in *London Calling*)

I look like an elderly wasp in an interesting
condition.

> Mrs Patrick Campbell (of the black and yellow
> costume for her part in *False Gods*)

He's miscast and she's Miss Taylor.

> Emlyn Williams (of Burton and Taylor
> in *Private Lives*)

I've seen Don entertain fifty times and I've always
enjoyed his joke.

> Johnny Carson

Lots of plays at the Royal Court are about people who talk away for hours and still can't communicate with each other.

Noël Coward

~·&·~

Drama critics are there to show gay actors what it is like to have a wife.

Hugh Leonard

~·&·~

The press is easier squashed than squared.

Winston Churchill

~·&·~

A critic is a man who knows the way but can't drive the car.

Kenneth Tynan

I approached reading his review the way some people anticipate anal warts.

Roseanne Barr

She's one great stampede from nose to navel.

Noël Coward (of an American columnist)

A censor is a man who knows more than he thinks you ought to.

Laurence J. Peter

It's the gossip columnist's business to write about what is none of his business.

Louis Kronenberger

By office boys, for office boys.

Lord Salisbury (of the *Daily Mail*)

~·§·~

No self-respecting fish would be wrapped in a Murdoch newspaper.

Mike Royko

~·§·~

You should always believe all you read in the newspapers, as this makes them more interesting.

Rose Macaulay

Every good journalist has a novel in him – which is an excellent place for it.

Russell Lynes

Journalism is unreadable, and literature is not read.

Oscar Wilde

A journalist has no ideas and the ability to express them.

Karl Kraus

Rock journalism is people who can't write interviewing people who can't talk for people who can't read.

Frank Zappa

Once a newspaper touches a story the facts are lost for ever, even to the protagonists.

Norman Mailer

The dawn of legibility in his handwriting has revealed his utter inability to spell.

Ian Hay (attrib.)

Only the names have been changed, to protect the guilty.

Noël Coward (of his short story *What Mad Pursuit*)

David Halberstam's book on the 1950s, called *The Fifties*, is as inspired and clever as its title.

John Podhoretz

An editor should have a pimp for a brother so he'd have someone to look up to.

Gene Fowler

Your manuscript is both good and original; but the part that is good is not original, and the part that is original is not good.

Samuel Johnson

This book fills a much needed gap.

Moses Hadas

～∙🐚∙～

The covers of this book are too far apart.

Ambrose Bierce

～∙🐚∙～

It was very intelligent and absolute rubbish.

Noël Coward (of a book written about his plays)

～∙🐚∙～

I have nothing to say, I am saying it and that is poetry.

John Cage

～∙🐚∙～

He is able to turn an unplotted, unworkable manuscript into an unplotted and unworkable manuscript with a lot of sex.

Tom Volpe (of Harold Robbins)

Although he tortures the English language, he has not yet succeeded in forcing it to reveal its meaning.

J.B. Morton

The work of a queasy undergraduate scratching his pimples.

Virginia Woolf (of James Joyce)

A louse in the locks of literature.

Alfred, Lord Tennyson (of a critic)

Very nice, though there are dull stretches.

Antoine de Rivarol (of a two-line poem)

I regard this novel as a work without any redeeming social value, unless it can be recycled as a cardboard box.

Ellen Goodman (of Danielle Steel's novel, *Message from Nam*)

Classic: a book which people praise and don't read.

Mark Twain

A writer of dictionaries, a harmless drudge.

Samuel Johnson

Shakespeare, Madam, is obscene, and, thank God, we are sufficiently advanced to have found it out.

Frances Trollope

The way Bernard Shaw believes in himself is very refreshing in these atheistic days when so many people believe in no God at all.

Israel Zangwill

Henry James was one of the nicest old ladies I ever met.

William Faulkner

This book is the best work of fiction since fidelity was included in the French marriage vows.

Rowan Atkinson

No one but a blockhead ever wrote, except for money.

Samuel Johnson

Discretion is not the better part of biography.

Lytton Strachey

In America only the successful writer is important, in France all writers are important, in England no writer is important and in Australia you have to explain what a writer is.

Geoffrey Cottrell

Should not the Society of Indexers be known as Indexers, Society of, The?

Keith Waterhouse

It's amazing how long it takes to complete something you're not working on.

R.D. Clyde

Get stewed; books are a load of crap.

Philip Larkin

When I want to read a novel, I write one.

Benjamin Disraeli

This obscure, eccentric and disgusting poem.

Voltaire

I never read a book before reviewing it; it prejudices a man so.

Sydney Smith

A freakish homunculus germinated outside lawful procreation.

Henry Arthur Jones (of George Bernard Shaw)

Always willing to lend a helping hand to the one above him.

F. Scott Fitzgerald (of Ernest Hemingway)

Booksellers are all cohorts of the devil; there must be a special hell for them somewhere.

Johann Goethe

For the reader who has put away comic books but isn't ready for editorials in the *Daily News*.

Gloria Steinem (of Jacqueline Susann's novel,
Valley of the Dolls)

Lloyd Webber's music is everywhere, but so is AIDS.

Malcolm Williamson

When Jack Benny plays the violin, it sounds as though the strings are still in the cat.

Fred Allen

Let's play a medley of your hit!

Oscar Levant (to George Gershwin)

Why do we have all these third-rate foreign conductors around when we have so many second-rate ones of our own?

Thomas Beecham

~·&·~

She was a singer who had to take every note above A with her eyebrows.

Montague Glass

~·&·~

It's one thing to want to save lives in Ethiopia, but it's another thing to inflict so much torture on the British public.

Morrissey (of the Band Aid concert)

Going to the opera, like getting drunk, is a sin that carries its own punishment with it.

Hannah More

Wagner's music is better than it sounds.

Mark Twain

Too many pieces of music finish too long after the end.

Igor Stravinsky

Jazz will endure, as long a people hear it through their feet instead of their brains.

John Philip Sousa

The tuba is certainly the most intestinal of instruments – the very lower bowel of music.

Peter de Vries

If one plays bad music people don't listen and if one plays bad music people don't talk.

Oscar Wilde

The English may not like music, but they absolutely love the noise it makes.

Thomas Beecham

He started life as a black boy; now he's a white girl.
Mary Frances Connelly (of Michael Jackson)

Prince looks like a dwarf who's been dipped in a bucket of pubic hair.

Boy George

Don't you stick your goddamned tongue out at me unless you intend to use it.

David Lee Roth

When Brahms is in extra good spirits, he sings, *The Grave is My Joy*

Tchaikovsky

An unalterable and unquestioned law of the musical world requires that the German text of French operas sung by Swedish artists should be translated into Italian for the clearer understanding of English speaking audiences.

Edith Wharton

He has Van Gogh's ear for music.

Orson Welles (of Donny Osmond)

Modern music is three farts and a raspberry, orchestrated.

John Barbirolli

The mama of Dada.

Clifton Fadiman (of Gertrude Stein)

A product of the untalented, sold by the unprincipled
to the utterly bewildered.

Al Capp (of abstract art)

There are only two styles of portrait painting; the
serious and the smirk.

Charles Dickens

A Realist is someone who paints what other people don't paint.

R.J. Richardson

～⁖～

Portrait painters tend to regard faces as not very still lives.

Alan Bennett

～⁖～

My art belongs to Dada.

Cole Porter (attrib.)

～⁖～

A tortoise-shell cat having a fit in a platter of tomatoes.

Mark Twain (on a Turner painting)

All the arts in America are a gigantic racket run by unscrupulous men for unhealthy women.

Thomas Beecham

Chapter 2

POLITICAL OPPOSITION

There but for the grace of God goes God.
                    Winston Churchill (of Stafford Cripps)

If they must stand up there on their soapboxes what else can they expect but to be knocked off? More scornful appraisals of the weaknesses and foibles of those who run the world.

Mr Speaker, I withdraw my statement that half the cabinet are asses – half the cabinet are not asses.

Benjamin Disraeli

We all know that Prime Ministers are wedded to the truth, but like other married couples they sometimes live apart.

Saki

I may not know much, but I know chicken-shit from chicken salad.

Lyndon B. Johnson (of a speech by Richard Nixon)

I think it will be a clash between the political will and the administrative won't.

   Jonathan Lynn and Anthony Jay, *Yes Prime Minister*

He is going around the country stirring up apathy.

   William Whitelaw (of Harold Wilson)

The Marxist law of distribution of wealth is that shortages will be divided equally among the peasants.

   John Guftason

The Vice-Presidency ain't worth a pitcher of warm spit.

   John Nance Garner

He played too much football without a helmet.
> Lyndon B. Johnson (of Gerald Ford)

Had he been a much worse man he would have done Canada much less harm.
> Sir Richard Cartwright (of John A. Macdonald)

He is a self-made man and worships his creator.
> Benjamin Disraeli (of John Bright)

Mon Général, si vous m'obstructerez, je vous liquiderai.
> Winston Churchill (to Charles de Gaulle),
> probably apocryphal

If voting changed anything they'd make it illegal.

Anon

He is forever poised between a cliché and an indiscretion.

Harold Macmillan

He is a sheep in sheep's clothing.

Winston Churchill (of Clement Attlee)

A Byzantine logothete.

Theodore Roosevelt (of Woodrow Wilson)

A sophisticated rhetorician, inebriated with the exuberance of his own verbosity.

Benjamin Disraeli (of William Gladstone)

It's a recession when your neighbor loses his job; it's a depression when you lose yours.

Harry S. Truman

His mind is a muskeg of mediocrity.

John Macnaughton

In war you don't have to be nice; you only have to be right.

Winston Churchill

～⁖～

He can compress the most words into the smallest ideas better than any man I ever met.

Abraham Lincoln

～⁖～

Christianity with a tomahawk!

Winston Churchill (of Lenin's philosophy)

～⁖～

Like being flogged with a warm lettuce.

Paul Keating (of an attack by the Opposition)

When the eagles are silent the parrots begin to jabber.

Winston Churchill

Politicians are like nappies – they should be changed regularly and for the same reason.

Patrick Murray

The juvenile lead.

Aneurin Bevan (of Anthony Eden)

A Conservative is a man who's too cowardly to fight and too fat to run.

Elbert Hubbard

Sir Stafford has a brilliant mind – until it is made up.

Violet Bonham Carter (of Stafford Cripps)

They are not fit to manage a whelk-stall.

Winston Churchill (of the British Labour Party)

Ronald Reagan is a triumph of the embalmer's art.

Gore Vidal

Fleas can be taught nearly anything that a Congressman can.

Mark Twain

Congressmen are so damned dumb, they could throw themselves on the ground and miss.

James Traficant

If the Republicans will stop telling lies about the Democrats, we will stop telling the truth about them.

Adlai Stevenson

There is only one thing worse than fighting with allies, and that is fighting without them.

Winston Churchill

So brilliant yet so corrupt, he shines and stinks like rotten mackerel by moonlight.

John Randolph (of Edward Livingston)

The word liberty in the mouth of Mr Webster sounds like the word love in the mouth of a courtesan.

· Ralph Waldo Emerson

It is not enough to have every intelligent person in the country voting for me – I need a majority.

Adlai Stevenson

He always played the game and he always lost it.

Winston Churchill (of Austen Chamberlain)

Ronald Reagan doesn't dye his hair, he's just prematurely orange.

Gerald Ford (attrib.)

Now that I am no longer President, I find that I do not win every game of golf I play.

George Bush

I don't think Kenneth Baker has a haircut, I think he just has an oil change.

Anon

I decided the worst thing you can call Paul Keating, quite frankly, is Paul Keating.

John Hewson

Greater love hath no man than this, that he laid down his friends for his life.

Jeremy Thorpe (of Harold Macmillan)

If Gladstone fell into the Thames, that would be a misfortune, and if anybody pulled him out, that, I suppose, would be a calamity.

Benjamin Disraeli

They couldn't pour piss out of a shoe if the instructions were written on the heel.

Lyndon B. Johnson

Clement Attlee is a modest little man with much to be modest about.

Winston Churchill

A politician will double cross that bridge when he comes to it.

Oscar Levant

Richard Nixon is the kind of politician who would cut down a tree then mount the stump to make a speech for conservation.

Adlai Stevenson

~ ⧫ ~

A curious mixture of geniality and venom.

Winston Churchill (of Lloyd George)

~ ⧫ ~

A politician will always be there when he needs you.

Ian Walsh

~ ⧫ ~

I cannot bring myself to vote for a woman who has been voice-trained to speak to me as though my dog had just died.

Keith Waterhouse (of Margaret Thatcher)

Clement Attlee reminds me of a dead fish before it has had time to stiffen.

George Orwell

He is a man suffering from petrified adolescence.

Aneurin Bevan (of Winston Churchill)

When they circumcised Herbert Samuel, they threw away the wrong bit.

David Lloyd George

Choosing between Bush, Clinton and Perot was like needing clean underwear but being forced to decide between three dirty pairs.

Michael Dalton Johnson

Politics is the conduct of public affairs for private advantage.

Ambrose Bierce

～·ⅰ̇·～

You're not an MP, you're a gastronomic pimp!

Aneurin Bevan

～·ⅰ̇·～

Politics is derived from two words – poly, meaning many, and tics, meaning small blood-sucking insects.

Chris Clayton

Democracy: the worship of jackals by jackasses.

H.L. Mencken

Washington couldn't tell a lie, Nixon couldn't tell the truth and Reagan couldn't tell the difference.

Mort Sahl

The Secret Service is under orders if Bush is shot, to shoot Quayle.

John Kerrey

A choice between the lesser of two weevils.

S.J. Perelman (of Gerald Ford and Jimmy Carter)

Military intelligence is a contradiction in terms.

Oswald G. Villard

In Pierre Elliott Trudeau, Canada has at last produced a political leader worthy of assassination.

Irving Layton

～'🔔.～

A dope with fat ankles.

Frank Sinatra (of Nancy Reagan)

～'🔔.～

Al Gore is in danger of becoming all things to no people.

Paul Bograd

～'🔔.～

Macaulay has occasional flashes of silence that make his conversations perfectly delightful.

Sydney Smith

He proves that no shirt is too young to be stuffed.

Larry Zolf (of Joe Clark)

Bill Clinton's foreign policy stems mainly from having breakfast at the International House of Pancakes.

Pat Buchanan

I wouldn't piss down Jerry Brown's throat if his heart was on fire.

James Carville

Nixon's philosophy was that if two wrongs don't make a right, try three.

Laurence J. Peter

~⚬~

I am opposed by all the short-haired women and the long-haired men in the Province.

Sir Rodmond Roblin

~⚬~

For Socialists, going to bed with the Liberals is like having oral sex with a shark.

Larry Zolf

~⚬~

They can kiss my rear end, if they can leap that high.

Pete Wilson

Ronald Reagan is remarkably fit, but he doesn't cup his hand to his ear as a sunshade.

Sam Donaldson

Dan Quayle taught the kids a valuable lesson: if you don't study you could wind up as Vice President.

Jay Leno

Chapter 3

BATTLE OF THE SEXES

Life after death is as improbable as sex after marriage.

Madeline Kahn

Men v women, women v men, marriage, divorce and a healthy batch of put-downs.

The useless piece of flesh at the end of a penis is called a man.

Jo Brand

His wife said she wanted an animal fur, so he bought her a donkey jacket.

Anon

Scratch a lover, and find a foe.

Dorothy Parker

I don't like all-in wrestling – if it's all in, why wrestle?

Mae West

~~·&·~~

If you're afraid of loneliness, don't marry.

Anton Chekhov

~~·&·~~

God made Adam before Eve because he didn't want any advice on the matter.

Patrick Murray

~~·&·~~

We don't take a sausage roll to a banquet.
Winston Churchill (in response to being asked why he hadn't taken his wife with him to Paris)

~~·&·~~

Familiarity breeds contempt – and children.

Mark Twain

Ask him the time and he'll tell you how the watch was made.

Jane Wyman (of ex-husband Ronald Reagan)

There standing at the piano was the original good time who had been had by all.

Kenneth Tynan

How many times do I have to flush before you go away?

Anon

The only difference about being married is that you don't have to get out of bed to fart.

Jimmy Goldsmith

Let's forget the six feet and talk about the seven inches.

Mae West

Fred Astaire was great, but don't forget that Ginger Rogers did everything that he did, backwards and in high heels.

Bob Thaves

A hard man is good to find.

Mae West

You stay here for a moment while I go up and fetch my etchings.

James Thurber

In Hollywood, marriage is a success if it outlives milk.

Rita Rudner

If only he'd wash his neck, I'd wring it.

Anon

Foreplay is like beefburgers – three minutes each side.

Victoria Wood

Brigands demand your money or your life; women require both.

Samuel Butler

∼·❦·∼

Women want mediocre men, and men are working hard to be as mediocre as possible.

Margaret Mead

∼·❦·∼

If I throw a stick will you leave?

Anon

∼·❦·∼

The only time a woman has a true orgasm is when she is shopping.

Joan Rivers

God created Adam lord of all living creatures, but Eve spoiled it all.

Martin Luther

Twenty million women rose to their feet with the cry "We will not be dictated to," and promptly became stenographers.

G.K. Chesterton (on Women's Lib)

Men are like car alarms – they both make a lot of noise no one listens to.

Diana Jordan

Another instance of the triumph of hope over experience.

Samuel Johnson (of the remarriage
of a widowed friend)

~ ❧ ~

Madam, don't you have any unexpressed thoughts?

George S. Kaufman

~ ❧ ~

My sex life is now reduced to fan letters from an elderly lesbian who wants to borrow $800.

Groucho Marx

~ ❧ ~

Women are more irritable than men, probably because men are more irritating.

Anon

You remind me of my brother – only he has a human head.

Judy Tenuta

When a man steals your wife, there is no better revenge than to let him keep her.

Sacha Guitry

Don't imagine you can change a man, unless he's in nappies.

Jasmine Birtles

Today's man: heart of gold, nerves of steel, knob of butter.

Anon

If men could get pregnant, abortion would be a sacrament.

Florynce Kennedy

~·&·~

The only way to get rid of cockroaches is to tell them you want a long term relationship.

Jasmine Birtles

~·&·~

All men are of the same mould but some are mouldier than others.

Anon

I suppose true sexual equality will come when a general called Anthea is found having an unwise lunch with a young, unreliable male model from Spain.

John Mortimer

A divorce costs much more than a wedding but it's worth it.

Anon

Divorce comes from the Latin word divorcerum meaning "having your genitals torn out through your wallet."

Robin Williams

Why should women mind if men have their faces on the money as long as we have our hands on it?

Ivy Priest

The weaker sex are the stronger sex because of the weakness of the stronger sex for the weaker sex.

Anon

If you think women are the weaker sex, try pulling the blankets back to your side.

Stuart Turner

I'm trying to imagine you with a personality.

Anon

We pondered whether to take a holiday or get a divorce, and we decided that a trip to Bermuda is over in two weeks, but a divorce is something you always have.

Woody Allen

The hardest task in a girl's life is to prove to a man that his intentions are serious.

Helen Rowland

Is it time for your medication or mine?

Anon

One of the most difficult things in this world is to convince a woman that even a bargain costs money.

Edgar Howe

~.§.~

One tongue is enough for a woman.

John Milton (when asked if his daughter was to learn any foreign languages)

~.§.~

Marriage is not all bed and breakfast.

R. Coulson

Instead of getting married again, I'm going to find a woman I don't like and give her a house.

Lewis Grizzard

Divorce is the best way of getting rid of a tiresome mother-in-law.

Anon

And the judge said "All the money and we'll shorten it to alimony."

Robin Williams

Macho does not prove mucho.

Zsa Zsa Gabor

~⋅⦂⚬⦂⋅~

The critical period in matrimony is breakfast time.

A.P. Herbert

~⋅⦂⚬⦂⋅~

At whatever stage you apologize to your wife, the answer is always the same: "It's too late now."

Denys Parsons

~⋅⦂⚬⦂⋅~

I married beneath me, all women do.

Nancy Astor

The feminine vanity case is the grave of masculine illusions.

Helen Rowland

English is called the mother tongue because father seldom gets a chance to use it.

Anon

Always suspect any job men willingly vacate for women.

Jill Tweedie

Marriage is an attempt to turn a night owl into a homing pigeon.

Anon

Il n'y a point de heros pour son valet de chambre.
No man is a hero to his valet.

Madame Cornuel

～🐝～

It isn't premarital sex if you have no intention of getting married.

Matt Barry

～🐝～

A good husband is one who will wash up when asked and dry up when told.

Anon

～🐝～

Every other inch a gentleman.

Rebecca West (of Michael Arlen)

The great secret of a successful marriage is to treat all disasters as incidents and none of the incidents as disasters.

Harold Nicholson

A good marriage would be between a blind wife and a deaf husband.

Michel de Montaigne

The most difficult year of marriage is the one you're in.

Anon

After a man is married he has the legal right to deceive only one woman.

Edgar Howe

Holy Deadlock.

A.P. Herbert

Men who put women on pedestals seldom knock them off.

Anon

No nice men are good at getting taxis.

Katharine Whitehorn

Not all men are annoying – some are dead.

Anon

Never trust a husband too far, nor a bachelor too near.

Helen Rowland

A widower enjoys a second wife as much as a widow enjoys her husband's life insurance.

Edgar Howe

A man has to do something to relieve the monogamy.

Anon

Madam, before you flatter a man so grossly to his face, you should consider whether or not your flattery is worth having.

Samuel Johnson

The female sex has no greater fan than I, and I have the bills to prove it.

Alan Jay Lerner

Give a man a free hand and he'll run it all over you.

Mae West

When she wears slacks she reveals stern facts.

Louis A. Safian

A plumber's idea of Cleopatra.

W.C. Fields (of Mae West)

A husband is what is left of a lover, after the nerve has been extracted.

Helen Rowland

A woman told me she would fulfill my ultimate fantasy for £100 – so I asked her to paint my house.

Sean O'Bryan

Chapter 4

THAT'S LIFE

If you think nobody cares whether you are alive
or dead, try missing a couple of car payments.
Ann Landers

*Some scathing statements and philosophical fillips on the
comedy of human living: money, religion, sport, people
and places (not without a smattering of xenophobia), food
and drink, age, health and death.*

It was one of those perfect summer days – the sun was shining, a breeze was blowing, the birds were singing and the lawnmower was broken.

James Dent

Life is a sexually transmitted disease.

Anon

How is it that the first piece of luggage on the airport carousel never belongs to anyone?

George Roberts

Life is something to do when you can't get to sleep.

Fran Lebowitz

The consumer isn't a moron; she is your wife.

David Ogilvy

～；❦；～

If you don't drink, smoke or drive a car, you're a tax evader.

Tom Foley

～；❦；～

Hardware is the part of the computer than can be kicked.

Jeff Pesis

～；❦；～

History is nothing but the soul's old wardrobe.

Heinrich Heine

～；❦；～

Never let the facts get in the way of a good story.

Anon

I got a letter from Princess Diana thanking me for taking her out of the headlines.

Graham Taylor

Sending men to that army is like shoveling fleas across a barnyard – not half of them get there.

Abraham Lincoln (of General McClellan's army)

You may know by my size that I have a kind of alacrity in sinking.

William Shakespeare

Every man has the right to be conceited until he is successful.

Benjamin Disraeli

～ ⟨●⟩ ～

I'm not tense, just terribly, terribly alert.

Anon

～ ⟨●⟩ ～

Perennials are the ones that grow like weeds, biennials are the ones that die this year instead of next and hardy annuals are the ones that never come up at all.

Katharine Whitehorn

～ ⟨●⟩ ～

I am determined to travel through life first class.

Noël Coward

All I need is room enough to lay a hat and a few friends.

Dorothy Parker

When Soloman said there was a time and a place for everything, he had not encountered the problem of parking an automobile.

Bob Edwards

A man described as a 'sportsman' is generally a bookmaker who takes actresses to night clubs.

Jimmy Cannon

Please don't ask me to relax – it's only the tension that's holding me together.

Helen Murray

Patience: a minor form of despair, disguised as a virtue.

Ambrose Bierce

A neurosis is a secret you don't know you're keeping.

Kenneth Tynan

I'm trusting in the Lord and a good lawyer.

Oliver North

I have a previous engagement which I will make as soon as possible.

John Barrymore (to an unwanted invitation)

As a football player at Princeton, I always felt like Dolly Parton's bra-straps – I knew I had an important job to do but I felt totally incapable of doing it.

Jimmy Stewart

Conscience is the inner voice which warns us that somebody may be looking.

H.L. Mencken

Genius is one per cent inspiration, ninety-nine per cent perspiration.

Thomas Alva Edison

If it squirms, it's biology; if it stinks, it's chemistry; if it doesn't work, it's physics and if you can't understand it, it's mathematics.

Magnus Pyke

One of the worst aspects of modern English life is that so many of one's friends have to work and they're so bad at it.

Noël Coward

Science is his forte, and omniscience his foible.

Sydney Smith (of William Whewell)

A gossip is one who talks to you about other people; a bore is one who talks about himself; a brilliant conversationalist is one who talks to you about yourself.

William King

He listens to his psychiatrist, and then draws his own confusions.

Anon

Keep a diary and some day it'll keep you.

Mae West

Good to eat, and wholesome to digest, as a worm to a toad, a toad to a snake, a snake to a pig, a pig to a man, and a man to a worm.

Mark Twain

Life is just one damned thing after another.

Elbert Hubbard

~·&·~

Good people sleep better than bad people, but bad people enjoy the waking hours much more.

Woody Allen

~·&·~

Life is a shit sandwich and every day you take another bite.

Joe Schmidt

~·&·~

I refuse to endure months of expensive humiliation only to be told that at the age of four I was in love with my rocking-horse.

Noël Coward

Early to bed and early to rise probably indicates unskilled labour.

John Ciardi

Assassination is the extreme form of censorship.

George Bernard Shaw

Imprisoned in every fat man a thin one is wildly signaling to be let out.

Cyril Connolly

Several excuses are always less convincing than one.

Aldous Huxley

Oh what a tangled web we weave, when first we practise to deceive.

Walter Scott

Seriousness is stupidity sent to college.

P.J. O'Rourke

History repeats itself; historians repeat each other.

Philip Guedalla

Orthodoxy is my doxy; heterodoxy is another man's doxy.

William Warburton

Haste is the mother of imperfection.

Anon

Excuse me, my leg has gone to sleep – do you mind if I join it?

Alexander Woollcott (to a person boring him at a party)

Hey, I didn't know you could get epilepsy without a brain.

Anon

A monstrous carbuncle on the face of a much-loved and elegant friend.

> Prince Charles (of an extension to the National Gallery, London)

~❧~

As guests go, you wish he would.

> Anon

~❧~

Aye, they say the new striker I'm opposing is fast – but how fast can he limp?

> Mick McCarthy

~❧~

I told him to take a picture of his testicles so he'd have something to remember them by if he ever hit me again.

> Bobby Knight

Thou whoreson zed! thou unnecessary letter!

William Shakespeare

He has impeccable bad taste.

Otis Ferguson

Did the aliens forget to remove your anal probe?

Anon

I never forget a face, but in your case I'll be glad to make an exception.

Groucho Marx

You blocks, you stones, you worse than senseless things!

William Shakespeare

He climbed the ladder of success kissing the feet of the one ahead of him and kicking the head of the one behind.

Anon

Why do you sit there looking like an envelope without any address on it?

Mark Twain

He never goes back on his word – without consulting his lawyer.

Anon

They claim to be he-men, but the hair from their combined chests wouldn't have made a wig for a grape.

Robert Benchley

He gets offended when others talk whilst he's interrupting.

Anon

Nothing is more responsible for the good old days than a bad memory.

Frank P. Adams

The more I read him, the less I wonder that they poisoned him.

Thomas Babington Macaulay (of Socrates)

I do desire we may be better strangers.

William Shakespeare

She walked across the ballroom as if she were trudging through deep snow.

Noël Coward

He's a real big gun – of small calibre and immense bore.

Anon

Never trust a man with short legs – brains too near their bottoms.

Noël Coward

If you're enjoying yourself in his company, it's all you're enjoying.

Anon

Unspeakable, like a hedgehog all in primroses.

Nancy Mitford (of Princess Margaret)

When there's nothing more to be said, he'll still be saying it.

Anon

He was dull in a new way, and that made many people think him great.

Samuel Johnson (of Thomas Gray)

∼ ⚬ ∼

He has a diarrhea of words and a constipation of ideas.

Anon

∼ ⚬ ∼

O hideous little bat, the size of snot.

Karl Shapiro

∼ ⚬ ∼

His egotism is a plain case of mistaken nonentity.

Anon

∼ ⚬ ∼

Sweep on, you fat and greasy citizens.

William Shakespeare (from *Antony and Cleopatra*)

He had a degree so he could ice cakes with joined-up writing.

A.A. Gill

I don't know why she has such objections to birth control; she's a living argument for it.

Anon

That indefatigable and unsavoury engine of pollution, the dog.

John Sparrow

It's a surprising how such a big head holds such a small brain.

Anon

~ ;&. ~

You're a parasite for sore eyes.

Gregory Ratoff

~ ;&. ~

The aristocracy is composed chiefly of asses – asses who talk about horses.

Heinrich Heine

~ ;&. ~

Jogging is for people who aren't intelligent enough to watch television.

Victoria Wood

My face looks like a wedding cake left out in the rain.

W.H. Auden

He lights up a room when he leaves it.

Anon

My genitals are a sort of travel version of Linford Christie's.

Frank Skinner

He lights up a room when he leaves it.

Have some tongue, like cures like.

Robert Yelverton Tyrrell
(to a boring dining companion)

He has attained such a depth of seediness that a flock
of starlings could feed off him.

Clive James

～ ⟨ ⟩ ～

When a bore leaves the room, you feel as if someone
came in.

Anon

～ ⟨ ⟩ ～

Would thou wert clean enough to spit upon.

William Shakespeare

Only dull people are brilliant at breakfast.

Oscar Wilde

I used to think the only use for sport was to give small boys something else to kick besides me.

Katharine Whitehorn

McEnroe . . . did his complete Krakatoa number.

Clive James

They say Tom Mix rides as if he's part of the horse, but they don't say which part.

Robert Sherwood

Golf is a good walk spoiled.

Mark Twain

Eamon D'Arcy has a golf swing like an octopus falling out of a tree.

David Feherty

The trouble with jogging is that by the time you realize you're not fit enough to do it, it's a long walk home.

Anon

The uglier a man's legs are, the better he plays golf – it's almost a law.

H.G. Wells

Ballesteros hits the ball further than I go on my holidays.

Lee Trevino

I'm playing golf like Tarzan and scoring like Jane.

Chi Chi Rodriguez

Colin Montgomerie has a face like a warthog licking piss off a stinging-nettle.

David Feherty

They should call it a swimming "ool" because the "p" is silent.

Patrick Murray

If you think it's difficult to meet new people, try picking up the wrong golf ball.

Jack Lemmon

❧

Like a Volvo, Borg is rugged, has good after-sales service and is very dull.

Clive James

❧

We don't need refs, but I guess white guys need something to do.

Charles Barkley

❧

This was the worst golf I ever played – I couldn't hit a cow's backside with a banjo.

David Llewellyn

I think Brian Moore's teeth are the kind you buy from a DIY shop and hammer in yourself – he's the only player we have who looks like a French forward.

Paul Rendall

Joggers are basically neurotic, bony, smug types who could bore the paint off a DC-10.

Rick Reilly

He loved to walk sideways towards them, like a grimly playful crab.

R.C. Robertson-Glasgow
(of George Gunn's bowling technique)

I do not participate in any sport that has ambulances at the bottom of the hill.

Erma Bombeck

I don't drop players – I make changes.

Bill Shankly

I don't think the discus will ever attract any interest
until we start throwing them at each other.

Al Oerter

Reality: a delusion created by an alcohol deficiency.

Anon

I saw a notice which said "Drink Canada Dry" so I've started.

Brendan Behan

All I can say is that I have taken more out of alcohol than alcohol has taken out of me.

Winston Churchill

It's always hard to see hope with a hangover.

P.J. O'Rourke

His favourite drink is the next one.

Anon

One more drink and I'd have been under the host.

Dorothy Parker

~·❦·~

There is no such thing as a small whiskey.

Oliver St John Gogarty

~·❦·~

You're not drunk if you can lie on the floor without holding on.

Dean Martin

~·❦·~

He goes into a bar optimistically and comes out misty optically.

Anon

~·❦·~

We drink one another's healths, and spoil our own.

Jerome K. Jerome

I always wake up at the crack of ice.

George E. Lewis

I'm only a beer teetotaler, not a champagne teetotaler.

George Bernard Shaw

Let's get out of these wet clothes and into a dry Martini.

Mae West

A woman drove me to drink and I never even had the courtesy to thank her.

W.C. Fields

But I'm not so think as you drunk I am.

J.C. Squire

Work is the curse of the drinking classes.

Oscar Wilde

A good rule is to state that the bouquet is better than the taste, and vice versa.

Stephen Potter

Look here, Steward, if this is coffee, I want tea; but if this is tea, then I wish for coffee.

Punch cartoon

Food is an important part of a balanced diet.

Fran Lebowitz

I go by tummy-time and I want my dinner.

Winston Churchill

Dinner possessed only two dramatic features – the wine was a farce and the dinner a tragedy.

Anthony Powell

Never serve oysters in a month that has no paycheck
in it.

P.J. O'Rourke

~·~

The cook was a good cook as cooks go; and as good
cooks go, she went.

Saki

~·~

When I ask for a watercress sandwich I do not mean a
loaf with a field in the middle of it.

Oscar Wilde

I went to a restaurant that serves "breakfast at any time" – so I ordered French Toast during the Renaissance.

Steven Wright

The murals in restaurants are about on a par with the food in art galleries.

Peter De Vries

The catch of the day was hepatitis.

Henny Youngman

The Hotel Carvery – as much gristle and cornflour as you can stuff down for a tenner.

A.A. Gill

I think a grave has walked over this goose.

Noël Coward

～ ¦▲¦ ～

This was a good dinner enough, to be sure; but it was not a dinner to ask a man to.

Samuel Johnson

～ ¦▲¦ ～

The baked potatoes looked like they had been excreted by a buffalo.

Brian Sewell

～ ¦▲¦ ～

I never drink water – look at the way it rusts pipes.

W.C. Fields

Whom the gods wish to destroy they first call promising.

Cyril Connolly

An expert is one who knows more and more about less and less.

Anon

No one with a specialty can hope to have a monopoly of it.

Mark Twain

However harmless a thing is, if the law forbids it most people will think it wrong.

W. Somerset Maugham

An uneasy conscience is a hair in the mouth.

Mark Twain

Success is the one unpardonable sin against our fellows.

Ambrose Bierce

We used to build civilizations; now we build shopping malls.

Bill Bryson

There's a big difference between free speech and cheap talk.

Anon

It takes more hot water to make cold water hot than it takes to make hot water cold.

Larry Dowd

Circumstances make man, not man circumstances.

Mark Twain

A boss is a person who's early when you're late and late when you're early.

Anon

Be not afraid of going slowly, only of standing still.

Chinese proverb

Culture: a thin veneer easily soluble in alcohol.

Anon

Existentialism means that no one else can take a bath for you.

Delmore Schwartz

Envy is an admission of inferiority.

Victor Hugo

Everyone sits in the prison of his own ideas.

Albert Einstein

Not in doing what you like best, in liking what you do is the secret of happiness.

J.M. Barrie

Scandal: something that has to be bad to be good.

Anon

Anger makes dull men witty, but it keeps them poor.

Francis Bacon

Cough and the world coughs with you, fart and you
fart alone.

Trevor Griffiths

It is impossible to enjoy idling thoroughly unless one
has plenty of work to do.

Jerome K. Jerome

Calamities are of two kinds: misfortune to ourselves,
and good fortune to others.

Ambrose Bierce

Humour is emotional chaos remembered in
tranquillity.

James Thurber

One of the most difficult things to give away is kindness – it is usually returned.

Anon

If you want the last word in an argument say: "I expect you're right."

Anon

You know what they say, if at first you don't succeed, you're not the only son.

Stephen Fry

If at first you don't succeed – you're fired.

Jen Graman

~ ❧ ~

A camel is a horse designed by a committee.

Alec Issigonis

~ ❧ ~

It was beautiful and simple as all truly great swindles are.

O. Henry

~ ❧ ~

A home keeps you from living with your parents.

P.J. O'Rourke

~ ❧ ~

The more one gets to know of men, the more one values dogs.

A. Toussenel

As one door closes, another slams in your face.

Rachel Heyhoe Flint

A door is what a dog is perpetually on the wrong side of.

Ogden Nash

Nothing is impossible for people who don't have to do it themselves.

Anon

On the day of victory, no fatigue is felt.

Arabic proverb

After you've heard two eyewitness accounts of an accident, it makes you wonder about history.

Dave Barry

The bridge to the future is the phallus.

D.H. Lawrence

A committee is an animal with four back legs.

John Le Carré

Mankind is divisible into two classes: hosts and guests.

Max Beerbohm

We ought never do wrong when people are looking.

Mark Twain

Absurdity: a statement of belief inconsistent with one's own opinion.

Anon

There is sufficiency in the world for man's need but not for man's greed.

Mahatma Gandhi

Better to keep your mouth shut and appear stupid than to open it and remove all doubt.

Mark Twain

～⁛～

If you don't believe in the resurrection of the dead, look at any office at quitting time.

Robert Townsend

～⁛～

The impossible: something that nobody can do – until somebody does it.

Anon

～⁛～

Don't let yesterday take up too much of today.

Will Rogers

Foolproof systems do not take into account the ingenuity of fools.

Gene Brown

Make three correct guesses consecutively and everyone will regard you as an expert.

Anon

There's only one thing in the world worse than being talked about and that is not being talked about.

Oscar Wilde

You will always find a few Eskimos ready to tell the Congolese how to cope with the heat.

Stanislaw Lec

It's a funny old world – a man's lucky if he gets out of it alive.

Walter de Leon and Paul M. Jones

Blessed is he who, having nothing to say, abstains from giving evidence of that fact.

George Eliot

A wit with dunces, and a dunce with wits.

Alexander Pope

He's just found a job that takes lots of guts – he strings tennis rackets.

Anon

The trouble with the rat-race is that even if you win, you're still a rat.

Lily Tomlin

All you need to grow fine, vigorous grass is a crack in your sidewalk.

James Hewett

A stingy person and a fat cow are useful only after they are dead.

Sholom Aleichem

There are only two types of exercise in Hollywood: jogging and helping a divorced friend move.

Robert Wagner

～｡～

America is one long expectoration.

Oscar Wilde

～｡～

Moscow is a city where, if Marilyn Monroe should walk down the street with nothing on but shoes, people would stare at her feet first.

John Gunther

What a pity it is that we have no amusements in England but vice and religion.

Sydney Smith

London! Dirty little pool of life.

B.M. Malabari

Poms don't have much imagination because they've pinched most of their street names off the Monopoly board.

Paul Hogan

England and America are two countries divided by a common language.

George Bernard Shaw

An Englishman, even if he is alone, forms an orderly queue of one.

George Mikes

❧

The Irish are a fair people; they never speak well of one another.

Samuel Johnson

❧

The best thing I know between France and England is – the sea.

Douglas Jerrold

❧

Afrikaans sounds like Welsh with attitude and emphysema.

A.A. Gill

California is a fine place to live – if you happen to be an orange.

Fred Allen

Life is too short to learn German.

Richard Porson

The French don't care what they do as long as they pronounce it properly.

George Bernard Shaw

I like my "abroad" to be Catholic and sensual.

Chips Channon

～•～

If ever there was an aviary overstocked with jays it is that Yaptown-on-the-Hudson called New York.

O. Henry

～•～

Poland is now a totally independent nation, and it has managed to greatly improve its lifestyle thanks to the introduction of modern Western conveniences such as food.

Dave Barry

～•～

Canadians are Americans with no Disneyland.

Margaret Mahy

At its worst, the broad Australian accent is reminiscent of a dehydrated crow uttering its last statement on life from the bough of a dead tree in the middle of a clay-pan at the peak of a seven-year drought.

Buzz Kennedy

Waiting for the German verb is surely the ultimate thrill.

Flann O'Brien

I once heard a Californian student in Heidelberg say, in one of his calmest moods, that he would rather decline two drinks than one German adjective.

Norway – the sun never sets, the bar never opens, and the whole country smells of kippers.

Evelyn Waugh

Britain has football hooligans, Germany has neo-Nazis and France has farmers.

Bernard Levin

Illegal aliens have always been a problem in the United States – ask any Indian.

Robert Orben

There are in England sixty different religious sects and only one sauce.

Caracciolo

It's where they commit suicide and the king rides a bicycle.

Alan Bennett (of Sweden)

I look upon Switzerland as an inferior sort of Scotland.

Sydney Smith

A soggy little island, always huffing and puffing to keep up with Western Europe.

John Updike

Of course America had often been discovered before Columbus, but it had always been hushed up.

Oscar Wilde

In India, "cold weather" is merely a conventional phrase and has come into use through the necessity of having some way to distinguish between weather which will melt a brass door knob and weather which only makes it mushy.

Mark Twain

American women expect to find in their husbands the perfection that English women only hope to find in their butlers.

W. Somerset Maugham

Americans love ice and hate cold water and so the swimming pools are as hot as bouillabaisse.

Noël Coward

The Japanese have perfected good manners and made them indistinguishable from rudeness.

Paul Theroux

German is the most extravagantly ugly language – it sounds like someone using a sick bag on a 747.

Willy Rushton

Belgium is a country invented by the British to annoy the French.

Charles de Gaulle

I know why the sun never sets on the British Empire:
God wouldn't trust an Englishman in the dark.

Duncan Spaeth

～⁖～

There is nothing the British like more than a bloke
who comes from nowhere, makes it and then gets
clobbered.

Melvyn Bragg

～⁖～

You cannot underestimate the intelligence of the
American people.

H.L. Mencken

～⁖～

There are only two classes of person in New South
Wales – those who have been convicted and those
who ought to have been.

Lachlan MacQuarie

Sydney is like Manchester with a harbour backdrop.

Robert Morley

The French are the masters of "the dog ate my homework" school of diplomatic relations.

P.J. O'Rourke

The perfidious, haughty, savage, disdainful, stupid, slothful, inhospitable, inhuman English.

Julius Caesar Scaliger

An Englishman's real ambition is to get a railway compartment to himself.

Ian Hay

If someone says: "It's not the money, it's the principle," it's the money.

Angelo Valenti

It's not that it is so good with money, but that it's so bad without it.

Anon

Money makes money and the money money makes makes money.

Benjamin Franklin

If economists were any good at business, they would be rich men instead of advisers to rich men.

Kirk Kerkorian

Adults are just kids who owe money.

Anon

A bank is a place that will lend you money if you can prove that you don't need it.

Bob Hope

I wish the banks would just say, "Look you ****, line up there, we don't give a **** about your miserable little bank account."

Paul Fussell

Prosperity is the best protector of principle.

Mark Twain

~ ❧ ~

When a man tells you he got rich by hard work, just ask him whose.

Anon

~ ❧ ~

The two most beautiful words in the English language are "Check Enclosed."

Dorothy Parker

~ ❧ ~

Death is the most convenient time to tax rich people.

David Lloyd George

I started out with nothing and I've still got most of it left.

Anon

Where there's a will there are relations.

Michael Gill

Business conventions are important because they demonstrate how many people a company can operate without.

J.K. Galbraith

Expenditure rises to meet income.

C. Northcote Parkinson

～⁙～

Some people go to church only when they are being baptized, married or buried – hatched, matched and dispatched.

James Hewett

～⁙～

It only rains straight down – God doesn't do windows.

Steven Wright

～⁙～

I am always most religious upon a sunshiny day.

Lord Byron

He prays on his knees on Sunday and on everybody the rest of the week.

Anon

It is no accident that the symbol of a bishop is a crook and the symbol of an archbishop is a double-cross.

Gregory Dix

The easy confidence with which I know another man's religion is folly teaches me to suspect that my own is also.

Mark Twain

God is a man, so it must be all rot.

Nancy Nicholson

God has Alzheimer's and has forgotten about us.

Jane Wagner

God will pardon me, it is His trade.

Heinrich Heine

Thanks to God, I am still an atheist.

Luis Buñuel

If God had meant us to walk around naked, he would never have invented the wicker chair.

Erma Bombeck

God is not dead but alive and working on a much less ambitious project.

Anon

Baptists are only funny underwater.

Neil Simon

God invented golf so white people would have an excuse to get dressed up like black people.

Stanley Morgan

Protestant women may take the pill whilst Catholic women must keep taking The Tablet.

Irene Thomas

～⁚🔔⁚～

A Christian is a man who feels repentance on a Sunday for what he did on Saturday and is going to do on Monday.

Thomas Ybarra

～⁚🔔⁚～

Maturity is a high price to pay for growing up.

Tom Stoppard

～⁚🔔⁚～

Old age isn't so bad when you consider the alternative.

Maurice Chevalier

By the time a person gets to greener pastures, he can't climb the fence.

Anon

Don't worry about senility – when it hits you, you won't know it.

Bill Cosby

Either he's dead, or my watch has stopped.

Groucho Marx

Two things grow weaker with the years – teeth and memory.

Anon

～·🔔·～

Excuse my dust.

Dorothy Parker (suggested epitaph)

～·🔔·～

To me old age is always fifteen years older than I am.

Bernard Baruch

～·🔔·～

Wrinkles merely indicate where smiles have been.

Mark Twain

～·🔔·～

I'm at the age where my back goes out more than I do.

Phyllis Diller

I got fired because of my age – I'll never make the mistake of being seventy again.

Casey Stengel

The report of my death was an exaggeration.

Mark Twain

Death is nature's way of telling you to slow down.

Anon

Memorial services are the cocktail party of the geriatric set.

Ralph Richardson

Here am I, dying of a hundred good symptoms.

Alexander Pope

Immortality is the condition of a dead man who does not believe he is dead.

H.L .Mencken

I have overcome my will-power and have taken up smoking again.

Mark Twain

Having smoking and non-smoking sections in the same room is like having urinating and non-urinating sections in a swimming pool.

Ross Parker

As a teenager you are in the last stage of life when you will be happy to hear that the phone is for you.

Fran Lebowitz

Drugs have taught an entire generation of English kids the metric system.

P.J. O'Rourke

If I wanted to hear the pitter patter of tiny feet I'd put shoes on my cat.

Anon

Even when freshly washed and relieved of all obvious confections, children tend to be sticky.

Fran Lebowitz

The only advantage to being an adult is that you can eat your dessert without have eaten your vegetables.

Lisa Alther

~·&·~

Teenagers are God's punishment for having sex.

Patrick Murray

~·&·~

Children are given us to discourage our better emotions.

Anon

~·&·~

Money isn't everything, but it sure keeps you in touch with your children.

J. Paul Getty

To be a successful father, there's one absolute rule: when you have a kid, don't look at it for the first two years.

Ernest Hemingway

It is not advisable to put your head around your child's door to see if it is asleep – it was.

Faith Hines

My mother loved children – she would have given anything if I had been one.

Groucho Marx

Telling a teenager the facts of life is like giving a fish a bath.

Arnold Glasow

～；🐚．～

Parents are the very last people who should be allowed to have children.

Anon

～；🐚．～

Ask your child what he wants for dinner only if he's buying.

Fran Lebowitz

～；🐚．～

Kids are like husbands – they're fine as long as they're someone else's.

Marsha Warfield

Some parents have difficulty deciding on a name for the new baby, but others have rich relatives.

Don McElroy

Always obey your parents, when they are present.

Mark Twain

Giving birth is not like shitting a melon – it's like excreting a block of flats, complete with patios, awnings, clothes-lines, television aerials, satellite dishes, backyard barbecues, kidney-shaped swimming pools, gazebos and double garage extensions with the cars parked outside.

Kathy Lette

I don't believe in smacking children – I just use a cattle prod.

Jenny Eclair

Perhaps host and guest is really the happiest relation for father and son.

Evelyn Waugh

Children despise their parents until the age of forty, when they suddenly become just like them, thus preserving the system.

Quentin Crewe

If that's mink she's wearing, some rabbit must be living under an assumed name.

Anon

Women give themselves to God when the devil wants nothing more from them.

Sophie Arnould

The "g" is silent – the only part of her that is.

Julie Burchill (of Camille Paglia)

She has a face like a well-kept grave.

Anon

Show me a woman who doesn't feel guilt and I'll show you a man.

Erica Jong

When women go wrong, men go right after them.

Mae West

Her once dangerous curves have become extended detours.

Anon

~·⚫·~

She looked as if she had been poured into her clothes and had forgotten to say when.

P.G. Wodehouse

~·⚫·~

She wears too much of not enough.

Anon

~·⚫·~

She has no heart but her brains are in the right place.

Cyril Asquith (of Diana Manners)

~·⚫·~

You say I'm a bitch like it's a bad thing.

Anon

A woman without a man is like a fish without a bicycle.

Gloria Steinem (attrib.)

She wears the kind of dresses that start late and end early.

Anon

A man without a woman is like a moose without a hat-rack.

Arthur Marshall

She knows how to hang on to her youth – she never introduces him to other women.

Anon

~··~

Outside every thin girl there's a fat man trying to get in.

Katharine Whitehorn

~··~

The only thing that can cheat her out of the last word is an echo.

Anon

~··~

The more underdeveloped the country, the more overdeveloped the women.

J.K. Galbraith

She finally admitted she was forty, but she didn't say when.

Anon

I refuse to admit that I'm more than fifty-two, even if that does make my sons illegitimate.

Nancy Astor

She dresses for the nuclear age – with fifty per cent fall out.

Anon

I wanted to marry her ever since I saw the moonlight shining on the barrel of her father's shotgun.

Eddie Albert

She's not what she was fifteen years ago – she's nine years older.

Anon

Some extraordinarily unlikely women do have it.

Noël Coward (on sex appeal)

She wears the kind of bikini that's based on the theory that nothing succeeds like nothing.

Anon

The best way for her to save face is to keep the lower half shut.

Anon

She looks like a million dollars – after taxes.

Anon

Englishwomen's shoes look like they were made by someone who had heard shoes described but had never seen any.

Margaret Halsey

She's a living example of stern reality – a plump dame in shorts.

Anon

Nobody loves a fairy when she's forty.

Arthur W.D. Henley

~·{·~

Underneath every successful man there's usually a woman.

Anon

~·{·~

She's aged more than her husband, but less often.

Anon

~·{·~

Don't get too friendly with her dear, or she'll make a nest in your hair.

Noël Coward

~·{·~

Well, this day was a total waste of make-up.

Anon

The best years of her life were the ten between twenty-nine and thirty.

Anon

Her hat looks as if it had made a forced landing on her head.

Anon

Old blondes never fade – they just dye away.

Anon

Chapter 5

JUST RIDICULOUS

There are just two rules for success: 1. Never
tell all you know.

Robert H. Lincoln

*A collection of bizarre sayings – the things we find funny
without really knowing why, as well as some "foot in
mouth" comments which their owners will have wished
they hadn't said.*

I'm going to memorize your name then throw my head away.

Oscar Levant

Where I come from, the valleys are so narrow that the dogs wag their tails up and down.

Sam Snead

The moon may be smaller than the earth, but it's further away.

Steven Wright

She's got more chins than the Hong Kong telephone directory.

Anon

If you get to be one hundred you've got it made – very few people die past that age.

George Burns

❧

I could see that, if not actually disgruntled, he was far from gruntled.

P.G. Wodehouse

❧

Two in every one people in this country are schizophrenic.

Anon

❧

Most people who are as attractive, witty and intelligent as I am are usually conceited.

Joan Rivers

A redneck died and left all his money to his wife —
she couldn't touch it until she was fourteen.

Jeff Foxworthy

He hasn't an enemy in the world, and none of his
friends like him.

Oscar Wilde (of George Bernard Shaw)

Does this condom make me look fat?

Anon

The Venus de Milo is a good example of what happens to somebody who won't stop biting her fingernails.

Will Rogers

I used to think that the human brain was the most fascinating part of the body and then I realized, "What is telling me that?"

"I digress," as the bride said when she got up in the middle of the night and baked a cake.

Noël Coward

If God had meant them to be lifted and separated, He would have put one on each shoulder.

Victoria Wood

Before I went to see *Deep Throat*, I thought it was a film about a giraffe.

Bob Hope

Passionate hatred can give meaning and purpose to an empty life.

Eric Hoffer

There is no housing shortage in England today – it's just a rumour put about by people who have nowhere to live.

G.L. Murfin

If I am ever stuck on a respirator or a life support system, I definitely want to be unplugged, but not until I get down to a size eight.

Henriette Mantel

Alas poor Yorlik, I knew him backwards.

Anon

I'm not bald – my head is just a solar panel for a sex machine.

Telly Savalas

Arnold Schwarzenegger looks like a condom full of walnuts.

Clive James

A bore: someone who talks when you want him to listen.

Ambrose Bierce

If the garbage man calls, tell him we don't want any.

Groucho Marx

I don't go to my psychiatrist any more – he was meddling too much in my private life.

Anon

Old MacDonald was dyslexic, IEIEO.

Billy Connolly

What's another word for Thesaurus?

Anon

Cocaine is God's way of saying you're making too much money.

Robin Williams

Reality is for people who can't face drugs.

Laurence Peter

I'd stay away from Ecstasy – it's a drug so strong it makes white people think they can dance.

Lenny Henry

Anybody who isn't pulling his weight is probably pushing his luck.

Anon

One of us must go.

Oscar Wilde (of the wallpaper which
he could see from his deathbed)

Obscenity is whatever gives the judge an erection.

Anon

He sneaked his girl out of the nudist camp because he
wanted to see what she looked like in a bathing suit.

Anon

Pedestrian: someone who thought he had petrol in his tank.

Anon

～⧯～

Policemen, like red squirrels, must be protected.

Joe Orton

～⧯～

Dolphins are so intelligent that within only a few weeks they can train a man to throw fish at them from the side of a pool.

Anon

～⧯～

Eyewitnesses were on the scene in minutes.

Adam Boulton

If Gloria hadn't divorced me she might never have become her own daughter-in-law.

Cy Howard (of his ex-wife who
married Howard's son)

First things first, second things never.

Shirley Conran

The only thing in my life that I regret is that I once saved David Frost from drowning.

Peter Cook

Like cannibalism, a matter of taste.

G.K. Chesterton

I learned law so well, the day I graduated I sued the college and got my tuition fees back.

Fred Allen

If incest is a relative bore and necrophilia is a dead bore, would you say that celibacy is never boring?

Anon

I would have killed myself but my analyst was a strict Freudian and if you kill yourself they make you pay for the sessions you miss.

Woody Allen

Ignorance of the law must not prevent the losing lawyer from collecting his fee.

John Mortimer

Recreations: growling, prowling, scowling and owling.

Nicholas Fairbairn's entry in *Who's Who*

This is the sort of English up with which I will not put.

Winston Churchill

Coincide: what you do when it starts raining.

Anon

The insurance man told me that I was covered for falling off the roof but not for hitting the ground.

Tommy Cooper

~•~

His psychiatrist is so expensive, all he gets for £25 is a get-well card.

Anon

~•~

There is no police like Holmes.

James Joyce

~•~

Does the name Pavlov ring a bell?

Anon

The quickest way to make a red light turn green is to try to find something in the glove compartment.

Gary Doney

I have nothing against the Jesuits but I wouldn't want my daughter to marry one.

Patrick Murray

I'm writing an unauthorized autobiography.

Steven Wright

I love flying – I've been to almost as many places as my luggage.

Bob Hope

$\sim \cdot \mathbf{\&} \cdot \sim$

It is like a barber's chair that fits all buttocks.

William Shakespeare

$\sim \cdot \mathbf{\&} \cdot \sim$

Any man who grows to be more than five feet seven inches is a weed.

Frank Lloyd Wright

$\sim \cdot \mathbf{\&} \cdot \sim$

I have always wanted to write a book that ended with the word "mayonnaise."

Richard Brautigan

Why is the alphabet in that order – is it because of that song?

Steven Wright

The key to tennis is to win the last point.

Jim Courier

I would rather read a novel about civil servants written by a rabbit.

Craig Brown (of *Watership Down*)

George Burns is old enough to be his father.

Red Buttons

I installed a skylight in my apartment and the people who live above me are furious!

Steven Wright

A mute told a deaf man how a blind man saw a cripple walk on water.

Anon

Researchers have already cast much darkness on this subject and if they continue their investigations we shall soon know nothing at all about it.

Mark Twain

Cross-country skiing is great if you live in a small country.

Anon

My theory of evolution is that Darwin was adopted.

Steven Wright

After twelve years of therapy my psychiatrist said something that brought tears to my eyes – he said, "No hablo ingles."

Ronnie Shakes

There's a fine line between fishing and standing on the riverside looking like an idiot.

Anon

There aren't enough days in the weekend.

Anon

~·&·~

A lot of people never use their initiative because nobody ever tells them to.

Mary Allen

~·&·~

If in the last few years you haven't discarded a major opinion or acquired a new one, check your pulse – you may be dead.

Anon

~·&·~

Smoking will cure weight problems . . . eventually.

Anon

I didn't suspect it was an orgy until three days later.

S.J. Perelman

I took a course in speed waiting – now I can wait an hour in only ten minutes.

Steven Wright

The world is like a cucumber – today it's in your hands, tomorrow it's up your arse.

Arab saying

Have you heard the one about the nudist who plays strip poker – every time he loses, he has to put something on.

Anon

～⋅⋅⋅～

I don't think God comes well out of it.

Virginia Woolf (on the Book of Job)

～⋅⋅⋅～

Is "tired old cliché" one?

Steven Wright

～⋅⋅⋅～

Backward ran sentences until reeled the mind.

Wolcott Gibbs

Just when you think tomorrow will never come, it's yesterday.

Anon

Aside from its purchasing power, money is useless as far as I'm concerned.

Alfred Hitchcock

People say that life is the thing, but I prefer reading.

Logan Pearsall Smith

Droughts are because God didn't pay his water bill.

Steven Wright

Never get into a narrow double bed with a wide single man.

Quentin Crisp

Give me a smart idiot before a stupid genius any day.

Samuel Goldwyn

What's wrong with being a boring kind of guy?

George Bush

I love California – I practically grew up in Phoenix.

Dan Quayle

Although he is a very poor fielder, he is a very poor hitter.

Ring Lardner

The IRA are indiscriminately killing men, women and children and now they have killed two Australians.

Margaret Thatcher

When it comes to ruining a painting, he's an artist.

Samuel Goldwyn

I would have given my right arm to have been a pianist.

Bobby Robson

⌣·¿·⌣

If we don't succeed, we run the risk of failure.

Dan Quayle

⌣·¿·⌣

I've never heard of this Greek chap Clitoris they're talking about.

Lord Albemarle

⌣·¿·⌣

I have my faults but being wrong isn't one of them.

Jimmy Hoffa

⌣·¿·⌣

Suicide is a real threat to health in a modern society.

Virginia Bottomley

One word sums up the responsibility of any Vice-President, and that word is "to be prepared."

Dan Quayle

A lot of people my age are dead at the present time.

Casey Stengel

It's more than magnificent, it's mediocre.

Samuel Goldwyn

A lot of horses get distracted – it's just human nature.

Nick Zito

If there's a pile-up in there, they'll have to give some of the players artificial insemination.

Curt Cowdry

～˙🐚˙～

Anything that man says you've got to take with a dose of salts.

Samuel Goldwyn

～˙🐚˙～

He'll regret it to his dying day, if ever he lives that long.

Frank Nugent

～˙🐚˙～

Jim Morrison is dead now and that's a high price to pay for immortality.

Gloria Estefan

I got up more nostrils than there are noses.

Andrew Neill

Anyone who goes to see a psychiatrist ought to have his head examined.

Samuel Goldwyn

I'm for a stronger death penalty.

George Bush

I read part of it all the way through.

Samuel Goldwyn

There's always a choice of whether one does it last week, this week or next week.

John Major

The new West Stand casts a giant shadow over the entire pitch even on a sunny day.

Chris Jones

~·¦⋅~

We are going to have the best educated American people in the world.

Dan Quayle

~·¦⋅~

I'll give it to you in two words: im possible.

Samuel Goldwyn

I want to make sure that everyone who has a job wants a job.

George Bush

We are not ready for any unforeseen event that may or may not occur.

Dan Quayle

For this part of a lady – somebody that's couth.

Samuel Goldwyn

We shall have no coal industry if the miners are driven into the ground.

Claire Brooks

The United States has much to offer the Third World War.

> Ronald Reagan (the mistake was repeated nine times in one speech)

~●~

Cauliflower is nothing but cabbage with a college education.

> Mark Twain

~●~

A friend is someone who will help you move; a good friend is someone who will help you move a body.

> Alexei Sayle

~●~

An Irish farmer, to cover the possibility of unexpected visitors, can often be found eating his dinner out of a drawer.

> Niall Toibin

Noël Coward's wartime letter to Lawrence of Arabia
(Aircraftsman T.E. Shaw, No. 338171):
Dear 338171, May I call you 338?

Free yourselves from the slavery of tea and coffee
and other slopkettle.

William Cobbett

I called my landlord and told him that my apartment
had terrible accoustics and he told me he'd caught
them all long before I moved in.

Anon

When the guy who made the first drawing board got it wrong, what did he go back to?

Steven Wright

Light pranks add zest to your services, but don't pull the customers ears.

Rules for Hotel Chambermaids, Japanese Tourist Board

A moose is an animal with horns on the front of his head and a hunting lodge wall on the back of it.

Groucho Marx

Bambi – see the movie! Eat the cast!

Henry Kelly

I've posed nude for a photographer in the manner of Rodin's *Thinker*, but I looked merely constipated.

George Bernard Shaw

The trouble with this business is the dearth of bad pictures.

Samuel Goldwyn

Nothing needs so reforming as other people's habits.

Mark Twain

Poets have been mysteriously silent on the subject of cheese.

G.K. Chesterton

Think of the old lady who had her petrol tank removed from her car and had it replaced with one that held litres instead of gallons.

Kenneth Manning

He's running a high temperature and his chest looks like a bad Matisse.

Noël Coward (of a friend with chicken pox)

A cucumber should be well sliced, and dressed with pepper and vinegar, and then thrown out, as good for nothing.

Samuel Johnson

Once, during Prohibition, I was forced to live for days on nothing but food and water.

W.C. Fields

Go and sing to them when the guns are firing – that's your job!

Winston Churchill (to Noël Coward)

Alcoholic: a man you don't like who drinks as much as you do.

Dylan Thomas

Nobody would wear beige to rob a bank.

Mickey Rose

A man could not be in two places at the same time unless he were a bird.

Sir Boyle Roche

~ ❧ ~

I phoned my local cab firm and said: "Can you please send me a big fat racist bastard with a personal hygiene problem some time before I have my menopause?"

Jo Brand

~ ❧ ~

If love is the answer, could you rephrase the question.

Lily Tomlin

~ ❧ ~

He that but looketh on a plate of ham and eggs to lust after it, hath already committed breakfast with it in his heart.

C.S. Lewis

Television is for appearing on, not looking at.

Noël Coward

Right now, I'm having amnesia and déjà vu at the same time. I think I've forgotten this before.

Steven Wright

Dwn wth vwls.

Ruth Ollins

Gossip: hearing something you like about someone you don't.

Earl Wilson

~·~

Every time I start to think the world is moving too fast, I go to the Post Office.

Anon

~·~

I'm giving you the chance to redeem your character, something you have irretrievably lost.

Serjeant Arabin QC

~·~

The single, overwhelming two facts were . . .

Paddy Ashdown

It's one of the great urban myths that people get pregnant in order to have children.

Menzies Campbell QC

The doctors X-rayed my head and found nothing.

Dizzy Dean

This is the worst disaster since I was elected.

Governor Pat Brown

I probably have a different sense of morality to most people.

Alan Clark

They pushed their nomination down my throat
behind my back.

J. Ramsay MacDonald

I am pro-life with exceptions, pro-choice with
limitations.

Senator John Warner

I am pro-life with exceptions, pro-choice with

When I want your opinion I'll give it to you.

Samuel Goldwyn

Make or break situations, such as we have seen here, can sometimes make as well as break.

Robin Oakley

I wear very simple shoes – it is not one of my weaknesses.

Imelda Marcos

I can't see who's in the lead but it's either Oxford or Cambridge.

John Snagge

Every Tom, Dick and Harry is called Arthur.

Samuel Goldwyn

The trouble with referees is that they just don't care which side wins.

Tom Canterbury

Did you get a good look at my face when I took your purse?

Accused thief who undertook his
own defense (and lost)

What's the plural of "ignited"?

Gaby Roslin

Everyone who is for abortion was at one time a faeces.

Peter Grace

A verbal contract isn't worth the paper it is written on.

Samuel Goldwyn

Chapter 6

SHARP RETORTS

Mahatma Gandhi was asked what he thought of
Western civilization:
I think it would be a very good idea.

*Snappy one-liners from (mostly) the rich and famous
which need a little explanation.*

Churchill was sent two tickets to the opening of George Bernard Shaw's new play with the message: Bring a friend – if you have one.

Churchill replied that he was otherwise engaged but would like to see the play's second performance: If there is one.

Calvin Coolidge, not known for his verbosity, was approached by a woman at a public function: Mr President, I have made a bet with my friends that I can make you say at least three words to me during dinner.

You lose, came the reply.

On hearing that a judge had slept through one of his plays, Richard Brinsley Sheridan commented:
Poor fellow, I suppose he fancied he was on the bench.

At a Hollywood party, the actress, Tallulah Bankhead met by chance an ex-lover whom she hadn't seen for years. She turned to him and said:
What are you doing here? I thought I told you to wait in the car!

Asked if he and his wife, Vita Sackville-West, had ever collaborated on anything, Harold Nicholson replied:
Yes, we have two sons.

When asked whether it was always sunny in Jamaica, Noël Coward answered:
Never at night.

Arguing against the necessity for a nation to be multilingual, Ralph Melnyk stated:
English was good enough for Jesus Christ.

Whilst in Egypt, T.E. Lawrence (Lawrence of Arabia) reluctantly attended a party hosted by a rather faded socialite who was famous for trying to befriend celebrities. Using the unseasonable hot weather as an opening, she sailed up to Lawrence saying:
92 today Colonel Lawrence! Imagine it! 92 today!
Many happy returns, madam, Lawrence replied.

During a speech to the United Nations, Khrushchev began banging his shoe on the desk, to which Harold Macmillan responded:

Perhaps we could have a translation, I could not quite follow.

On learning from Robert Benchley that Calvin Coolidge had died, Dorothy Parker asked: How could they tell?

He had an erection, retorted Benchley.

During a speech, the politician Robert Menzies was heckled by a lady in the audience who shouted: I wouldn't vote for you if you were the Archangel Gabriel!

Without hesitation, Menzies replied: If I were the Archangel Gabriel, madam, you would scarcely be in my constituency.

Harold Nicholson was telephoned by the *Sunday Express* who wanted to know what was his wish for that year. He replied:

Not to be telephoned by the *Sunday Express* when I am busy.

John Wilkes was told by a voter that he would rather vote for the devil than for Wilkes. The politician replied:

And if your friend is not standing?

When asked if he believed in God, Noël Coward answered:
We've never been intimate.

Thomas Beecham heard that Malcolm Sargent, whose nickname was "Flash Harry" was conducting concerts in Japan. He commented:
Ah – Flash in Japan!

Whilst Noël Coward was in Australia, a gushing fan rushed up to him and asked him to say something funny to her. He leaned and whispered loudly in her ear:
Kangaroo!

On his deathbed, Voltaire was urged by a priest to renounce the devil. He protested:
This is no time for making new enemies.

When asked in an interview how his autobiography was progressing, Noël Coward replied:
Absolutely limping.

W.C. Fields was asked why he never drank water.
Because fish fuck in it.

Asked why he had made a commercial for American Express, Peter Ustinov answered:
To pay for my American Express.

As the playing of the orchestra began to improve, Thomas Beecham commented to violinist Jean Pougnet:
Don't look now M. Pougnet, but I think we're being followed.

It was eight in the evening when George S. Kaufman was asked, in the form of an invitation, what was he was doing for dinner that night.
Digesting it.

The jazz musician, Zoot Sims, was asked how he could play so well when he was loaded.
I practice when I'm loaded.

Arnold Toynbee, author of *A Study of History*, which took him thirty-five years to complete, was asked by a journalist what had impelled him to devote that amount of time to a single work.
Curiosity.

Groucho Marx was asked if Groucho was his real name. He replied:
No, I'm breaking it in for a friend.

Did you mail that check to the judge?
Roy M. Cohn (in public, to his assistant)

Noël Coward was with a group of friends when someone announced that a boorish and overbearing acquaintance had "blown his brains out," to which Coward retorted:

He must have been an incredibly good shot.

When a waiter spilled soup on her dress, Beatrice Lillie complained:

Never darken my Dior again.

Alan Clark was asked by Douglas Hogg, then a junior Whip, how he was "keeping the new boys in order." He responded:

By offering them your job.

During his speech, President William Howard Taft complained that there was so much noise in the audience he could hardly hear himself talk, to which someone at the back replied:

It's OK, you're not missing anything.

On being told that his fly buttons were undone Winston Churchill said:

No matter – the dead bird does not leave the nest.

Noël Coward was asked what sort of a child he had been:

When paid lots of attention, extremely lovable; when not, a pig.

In explanation of his dire performance in his Civil Service examinations John Maynard Keynes said:
I evidently knew more about economics than my examiners.

George S. Kaufman, drama editor of the *New York Times*, was asked by an agent how they could get their leading actress's name into his newspaper.
He replied: Shoot her.

Rebecca West discovered in 1945 that her name, along with Noël Coward and other luminaries, had been on the Nazi blacklist. Discussing it with Coward she commented:
Just think who we'd have been seen dead with!

Frank Underhill was asked how he could vote Liberal:
I just hold my nose and mark the ballot.

When asked, while an undergraduate at Oxford, what he did for his college, Evelyn Waugh responded:
I drink for it.

When Senator Wyche Fowler was asked whether he had ever smoked marijuana, he replied:
Only when committing adultery.

Bessie Braddock: Winston you are drunk.
Winston Churchill: Madam you are ugly, but I shall be sober in the morning.

William Gladstone: I am convinced that you will die either of a pox or on the gallows.
Benjamin Disraeli: That depends sir, on whether I embrace your mistress or your principles.

Tallulah Bankhead was asked by a male journalist if she had ever been mistaken for a man. Her reply:
No darling, have you?

Rejection slip for a poem entitled "Why Do I Live?"
Because you send your poem by mail.

Eugene Field

An actress, worried about aging, confided to a friend that she dreaded the thought of forty-five. The "friend" asked: Why, what happened then?

Singer: You know, I insured my voice for fifty thousand dollars.
Conductor: Really, and what did you do with the money?

Performers' responses to hecklers:

Your parents are siblings, right?

If I wanted any shit from you, I'd squeeze your head.

Look, this is my job – I don't turn up at your work and spit on the burgers.

Let me guess – tonight's square dance was cancelled, right?

Dost thou jeer and flout me in the teeth?
William Shakespeare

Peace, ye fat guts.

William Shakespeare

Away, thou issue of a mangy dog!

William Shakespeare

And put-downs:

I enjoyed your book , who wrote it for you?
Darling, I'm so glad you liked it. Who read it to you?

How about coming back to my place?
Will two people fit under a rock?

Hey gorgeous, how do you fancy a good time?
Sorry, I don't date outside my species.

How do you like your eggs in the morning?
Unfertilized.

Is your husband a bookworm?
No, just an ordinary one.

Is your husband a bookworm?

No woman ever made a fool of me.
Who did then?

All's well that ends well – and vice versa.

Anon